Lin's Uncommon Life

written by Scott Shackelford & Emily Castle
illustrated by Hannah Dickens

WELL HOUSE
BOOKS

This book is a publication of

Indiana University Press

Office of Scholarly Publishing
Herman B Wells Library 350
1320 East 10th Street
Bloomington, Indiana 47405 USA

iupress.org

Manufactured in the United States of America

First Printing 2023

Cataloging information is available from the Library of Congress.
ISBN 978-0-253-06581-0 (cloth)
ISBN 978-0-253-06583-4 (ebook)

For Lin.
Your life and work has inspired us all.

Lin woke up early. She usually did. Lin liked to lie in bed listening to music playing on the radio downstairs. It filled the house, and her heart, as she thought about the day ahead.

Lin walked downstairs and saw her dad sitting at the dining room table.

"What's that, Dad?" Lin asked.

2

"Good morning sweetie! It's a model for a new musical," her dad said. "We're moving lots of dirt and planting a little forest to make it look real."

"Neat," Lin said. She thought to herself that she liked the look of the scene with trees and flowers. There was something about nature that called to her. She wanted to understand it, to cherish it.

Lin grew up many years ago in Beverly Hills, California. She lived in a house with a big backyard. There were fruit trees and lots of space for a garden. Lin's family grew their own vegetables. It made Lin feel independent. She liked solving her own problems.

When Lin was seven, her parents got divorced. It was a sad, confusing time. Lin and her mom moved into an apartment away from their big backyard. One bright spot was Lin's grandmother. They loved baking cookies together.

Moving meant **Lin went to a new school.** It was in the fancy part of town. The other kids lived in big houses and wore nice clothes. Sometimes, Lin felt out of place in her simple clothes. She was also embarrassed by how she spoke. Lin had a stutter. This made it hard for her to get the words she wanted to say out.

BHHS

When Lin was in high school, a teacher saw past Lin's stutter to something special inside. The teacher said to Lin, "You're smart. I know how to help with that stutter. Join the debate team!"

After a lot of hard work, Lin was a debating champion! She learned important lessons: There are two sides to every argument. You need to defend your ideas. And it is important to see where the other person is coming from. Lin was not going to let a stutter hold her back.

Lin graduated at a time when most girls did not go to college, unlike today. But, thanks to Lin's good education, **she knew that was the path for her!**

FILM

graduation day

loma of Graduation

Lin enjoyed college and did well. After college, Lin got married. She worked while her husband continued in school. Lin was very good at her job, but she wanted to do more. She started to think about going back to school herself. Like her parents, Lin and her husband decided to get divorced. They realized that they wanted different things out of life.

9

Lin decided to return to school. She wanted to study economics. But back when she was in high school, she had not been able to take the math classes she needed. Instead, she entered the political science program.

Through the years, **Lin learned not to get frustrated when things did not go her way.** Unfortunately, this included when she wasn't treated equally and was not allowed to take harder math classes in school because she was a girl. Lin found another way by teaching herself the math and studying a different subject.

While in school, **Lin met an interesting professor named Vincent Ostrom.** She got to know Vincent better, and they fell in love and got married. Together they began what would become a lifetime of **contestation**—which means debating and working together.

While Lin finished school, Vincent was offered a job at **Indiana University**.

ROUTE 66

HOLLYWOOD

California

★ Ucla

GREAT LAKES

The small town of **Bloomington** was in the forests of southern Indiana. It had a lot of nature to explore and appealed to both of them.

Chicago

ROCKY MOUNTAINS

"Should we visit?" asked Vincent. "Yes!" said Lin.

IU

ANA

Vincent's job was in the Department of Political Science. Many colleges wouldn't hire women to teach in the 1960s.

But IU did. In 1965 they made Bloomington their new home.

The first class Lin taught met at an unpopular time—Saturday mornings. But Lin had tons of energy and loved teaching others. She made the class fun and inspired the students by her example.

One day Lin said to Vincent: **"I like it here, but I feel like we could be doing more.** There are big issues I want to work on. But I don't think we have a way to do that."

"What are you thinking?" asked Vincent.

"In class we talk about how people can accomplish a lot when they work together," said Lin. **"Let's create a place where people can ask hard questions.** Where they can share their unique strengths and experiences."

"Like a research center?" asked Vincent.

Lin remembered the night before when she and Vincent worked with their friend Paul to make furniture.

"Research is like building furniture," said Lin. "This should be a place to experiment. A place to come together and solve problems. Why don't we call it a workshop? After all, scholarship is craftsmanship."

In 1973, they opened their Workshop! This welcoming community allowed them to tackle real-world problems. They weren't afraid to try out new ideas. Groundbreaking research followed.

In the 1970s, for example, people thought that bigger was always better. Bigger police departments. Bigger hospitals. Bigger schools. Lin wasn't so sure. She studied the Indianapolis Police Department. Her research found that in this case, the small police departments often did better than the bigger ones and built better relations with the community. Lin's findings showed that she was onto something important.

"I wonder…this idea of smaller is better, could it be happening in other places?" asked Lin. "I think we should see how communities around the world deal with their problems."

"You mean, you'd like to study the tragedy of the commons?" asked Vincent.

The tragedy of the commons was an idea that people are not good at sharing things others need, like drinking water. Instead, they take as much as they can for their use only.

Picture a village with a grassy field in the middle. The villagers use the field so their sheep can graze. Soon the sheep eat all of the grass, and there is no more grass to share.

To save the field, people think that either a government needs to create rules, or the field should be divided with a part going to each villager. But Lin wasn't convinced. "What if there's a third way?"

Lin, with Vincent, other collaborators, and students, traveled the world to answer that question. They went to Nepal. They went to Mexico. They traveled through Africa and Asia.

And everywhere Lin went, she found that communities do create rules. They do this to make sure everyone has enough to eat and drink. People can work together to share the water and forests.

Trust is the most important resource! Lin thought.

23

Governing the Commons

AND HOW TO MANAGE THEM

Lin saw similar behavior all over the world. She wrote about these stories in a book called *Governing the Commons*.

HOW TO SHARE
A COMMON RESOURCE

ONE

Say what is being shared,
where it is, and who is
allowed to use it.

TWO

Let the whole group help
make the rules for using
the item.

THREE

Watch behavior and punish
rule breakers.

FOUR

Problems should be solved
fairly and quickly.

GOVERNING
the COMMONS

ELINOR OSTROM

The book was published in 1990. It helped to inspire a new generation of students to follow Lin's example. This was the first of many books that Lin wrote.

Lin researched and taught for the next nineteen years. She worked with others around the world and improved her ideas. **Lin always stayed curious.**

Then one day, Lin's hard work was rewarded with a great honor. In the early morning of October 12, 2009, Lin received a phone call from Stockholm, Sweden.

"Hello?" said Lin.

"Good morning. May I speak to Elinor Ostrom please?"

"Yes, this is her speaking," replied Lin.

"Hello, my name is Adam Smith. I'm calling from the Nobel Foundation in Stockholm. It is my great honor to inform you that you have been awarded the prize in Economic Sciences."

Lin was shocked. She had just won the prestigious Nobel Prize for her research!

"Well, it's an unbelievable honor!" said Lin to Adam. "I lived through an era where I was discouraged from going to graduate school. People thought I would teach, but never do important research. Ah ha ha, life has changed!"

Lin had spent much of her career studying the field of the commons, yet her life was anything but common.

Lin was both the first woman and first political scientist in history to win the Nobel Prize in Economic Sciences!

Lin devoted her life to coming up with new ieas. She and Vincent made their own special path. They created a community, a Workshop. Even today, this community is working to make a better world for all of us.

Lin's life was uncommon. But her journey need not be.

You can walk in Lin's footsteps and forge your own path. Make sure to follow your dreams, and don't let others stand in your way. Find wonder in the simple things. Do what you can to help others. And, as Lin always did, think globally but act locally. The small steps we all take, from recycling to planting a tree, add up to make a big difference.

As Lin said:

"Little by little, BIT BY BIT, family by family, so much good CAN BE DONE ON so many levels."

Lin's Uncommon Life

1919
September 25 –
Vincent Ostrom is born

1933
August 7 –
Elinor Awan is born

1951
Lin graduates from Beverly Hills High School

1954
Lin graduates with a B.A. in political science from UCLA

1962
Lin graduates with an M.A. in political science from UCLA

1963
Lin and Vincent get married

1965
Lin graduates with a Ph.D. in political science from UCLA (dissertation title, "Public Entrepreneurship: A Case Study in Ground Water Basin Management")

Lin and Vincent move to Bloomington, Indiana; Lin joins the IU faculty as a visiting assistant professor

1967

Lin and Vincent begin building a cottage on Manitoulin Island in Canada that will serve as their summer writing retreat

1973

Lin and Vincent create the Workshop in Political Theory and Policy Analysis at IU

1990

Governing the Commons is published

1970s

Lin and Vincent begin an apprenticeship with Bloomington cabinetmaker Paul Goodman to make furniture for their house

1993

Institutional Incentives and Sustainable Development is published

1972

Lin studies the functions of the Indianapolis Police Department

1994

Rules, Games, and Common-Pool Resources is published

1999

Lin is the first woman to receive the prestigious Johan Skytte Prize in Political Science

2003

Trust and Reciprocity is published

2005

Understanding Institutional Diversity is published

2009

Lin is the first woman to win the Nobel Memorial Prize in Economic Sciences

2012

June 12 —
Lin passes away
June 29 —
Vincent passes away

2010

Lin is elevated to the rank of Distinguished Professor at IU; Lin and Vincent receive the University Medal

2020

A statue honoring Lin is added to the IU Bloomington campus, the first statue of a woman in the university's 200-year history

Elinor (Lin) Ostrom lived a life filled with hard work, travel, and friendship, breaking down barriers wherever she went. From overcoming childhood hardships, she became the first woman to win the Nobel Prize in Economic Sciences.

This is the story of her uncommon life!

Scott Shackelford is Executive Director of both the Ostrom Workshop and the Center for Applied Cybersecurity Research and Professor of Business Law and Ethics at the Indiana University Kelley School of Business.

Emily Castle is Assistant Director and Librarian of the Ostrom Workshop at Indiana University Bloomington.

Hannah Dickens is a graphic artist passionate about animation, illustration, and finding anything and everything secondhand. She calls the Midwest home with her husband, daughter, and rescue pets (a Labrador retriever and a parrot).